Top Ten Crises

For Survivalist And Preppers

by Tristan Trubble

Published in USA by:

Tristan Trubble
P.O BOX #9
Boynton Beach
FL 33425

© Copyright 2016

ISBN-13: 978-1540328588
ISBN-10: 1540328589

Table of Contents

Introduction

In the survival community there are basically two categories of people involved. There are the splinter cell sorts, which consist of people prepping for a very specific set of events, and there are those that are trying to prep for every possible crisis imaginable. Within those two categories are various levels of participation. There are individuals who are very meticulous, in depth and sticklers for adhering to detail. There are middle of the pack preppers, which consists of those individuals currently working towards a specified goal, yet their prepper plans remain incomplete, and a work in progress. Then you have the armchair preppers, which consist of people who know every survival skill and prepper program on the planet. They are willing to share their thoughts and ideas with you whenever possible, usually by telling you what they would do different, even though they have never participated in anything they are trying to preach.

The reasons people begin prepping is because they have come to the understanding that the world as we once knew it is constantly changing. Population levels continue to increase exponentially, and manmade disasters are now almost as common as natural ones. If you have found yourself coming here looking for pertinent information on a given survival subject, then you likely have found yourself developing a concern about the possibility of a catastrophe compromising the safety and security of you and your family members. Once you get involved with prepping, you will realize that the only reason you were concerned in the first place was because you weren't prepared for the worst. When you are prepared to handle anything and everything that comes your way, fear vanishes and confidence replaces it.

The main reasons people begin prepping is to accommodate for any number of disaster related scenarios. These reasons can change in level of importance depending on the current conditions. The top 10 concerns we will cover here are not displayed in descending order according to degree of importance, or potential of occurrence. It is really a very difficult process to try and identify the topics on this list in such a fashion, since we all live in different regions, under various conditions, with different numbers of members in the survival party, and with different ideas on what matter is the most pressing.

An Economic Collapse

This is one of the top 10 crisis conditions several people are focusing on in the present day. We have witnessed to economic collapse of a few international countries already, and many people believe that America is on the precipice of such a catastrophe in the very near future. In order to survive a financial collapse situation, you should begin diversifying your investment portfolio with an emphasis on converting what capital you can into precious metals, gems, jewelry and high priority bartering and trade items.

The United States has recently experienced a partial government shutdown, and in the process several EBT card systems were knocked off line. This resulted in small pockets of civil uprising, but sent a very serious shockwave through the financial community, by alerting Americans as to what a nationwide situation of a similar nature might entail.

It should also be noted that the US Dollar is in rapid decline. China has positioned itself to propose that the rest of the international community consider absolving the US Dollar as the international monetary reserve capital. If/when that happens, the value of the US Dollar will plummet, spiraling miserably out of control and depositing the US economy in the global cellar, so to speak.

This is an area you should probably begin focusing on as soon as possible. The US Dollar is a fiat currency system. The paper money we use has a value attached to it that is based of faith. In other words, it only works as long as people believe it is worth the denomination printed on it. There is no intrinsic value associated with it, which in laymen's terms, makes it as valuable as pocket lint. Eventually this will become evident to the rest of the world, and life as we know it in this country will change. There will likely be a lengthy transition system as the American citizens begin to develop a new currency system that will function on the international market. When that happens, precious metals, gems, jewelry and bartering items of significant value will be the primary methods of payment accepted for transactions.

You should consider investing in valuable **coined currency** that has verifiable precious metal content. Be wary and be wise in this endeavor as there are counterfeit coins in circulation that appear valuable yet really have no real value. Look for the purest, high quality content coins. Older American coins that contain silver or gold will be valuable, as will other fractionated international coins. Stay away from plated products as the only value with these is in the coating material. The internal metal is usually junk and not worth its own weight.

A Social Collapse

This is another disaster scenario a lot of people are starting to consider a very real possibility here in America. We have witnessed civil uprisings, civil wars, and international conflicts, all of which have had a devastating impact on the local population and societal infrastructures. In America, our current political atmosphere, and continued loss of respect on the international scene, has made several people extremely nervous about our own society collapsing, in multiple small pockets, or as an entire nation. There are several groups, organizations and militias that have all begun to become more and more aggressive in their approaches to protesting and issuing grievances. We have even witnessed individuals act out aggressively towards the established governments, federal, state and local, so it is not unreasonable to assume that the scales could tip dramatically at any moment.

Social collapse situations can have some very damaging consequences, nationally as well as internationally. Civil unrest, uprisings, protests and a base belief that government is not working in the interest of the people they govern. A second civil war could be a consequence of abusive government practices. With that comes the very real possibility of Martial Law being enacted, as well as the very real possibility that the United States would be invaded by an international adversary, or coalition. We could find ourselves in the very same type of situation as many Middle East countries currently fighting internal and external turmoil simultaneously.

Surviving a social collapse situation will be an exercise in self-reliance and sufficiency. If Martial law or foreign invasion is part of the situation, bugging out to an established bunker, or safe haven complex will be a very important aspect, and more than likely the very first thing you will need to do in order to prevent being rounded up and carted off to a relocation center/ concentration camp. This is something that could last for days, weeks, months or years, so preparations need to be in place long before this occurs.

Very specific **survival skills** will need to be learned, practiced and implemented in order to make it through this type of ordeal. Supplies will need to be stocked, gardening and livestock rearing will need to be addressed. Tactical response to invaders and operations security will need to be discussed and implemented. Communications will also be an area requiring focus and attention. You will need items to barter with, guns to hunt with as well as protect yourself with, and you may have to be constantly on the move in order to avoid detection and imprisonment.

Martial Law and FEMA Camps

This is something that could occur, with or without a civil uprising, or social collapse setting. The current political climate and atmosphere in America is ripe with signs that the federal and state levels of government are getting themselves prepared for something of epic proportions.

The DHS (Department of Homeland Security) has basically morphed into a national militarized police force. They have purchased ammunition and assault rifles in bulk, giving very little logical, or reasonable explanations for this sudden massive purchase of death dealing equipment. At the same time, the federal government under the Obama administration continues to push for stricter gun control, signing unconstitutional UN Arms

Treaties and agreements, in direct opposition to what the American population wants, or what the Constitution allows.

FEMA is an agency that was supposedly set-up to assist areas adversely affected by natural or manmade disasters. They are also an agency in charge and control of several camps around the country, which are called "Residential Relocation Centers." Anyone that has seen these establishments in person claims they are anything but a friendly environment designed to protect the population being kept inside. They have the very authentic look of modern day WWII Nazi prisoner camps.

The Obama administration has shown no mercy in their approach to dismantle the Constitution by signing several Executive Orders to basically assume control over all forms of American infrastructure at will, and without warning. They exhibited their potential for using them during the October 2013 partial government shutdown, closing National Parks and monuments by spending more to barricade them than it would've cost to simply leave them open. These places required little to no supervision, yet were staffed with armed guards and barricades to prevent the public from viewing, enjoying and appreciating these historical artifacts. This was seen by many as an indication of just how far the federal government was willing to go try and make the public revolt so that Martial Law could indeed be implemented. While that may be a conspiracy theory, the evidence speaks for itself and shows that the federal government will spare no expense to try and control the actions of the people they govern.

In order to survive a Martial Law scenario, you will need to learn several of the survival skills required for surviving an economic and/or social collapse. Keeping off the beaten path and **<ins>remaining invisible</ins>** will be a top priority. There will be all kinds of chaos, turmoil and people trapped in the mess. People may be rounded up and relocated, some will undoubtedly head for the hills, half-prepared, the other half simply hopeful. There may be small skirmishes and battles taking place depending on location and personal preference for surviving and resisting.

An EMP Strike

This is something that could happen as a result of natural or manmade disaster. Some members of the scientific community claim that Earth is long overdue a blast of solar energy from our solar system's life supporting star, the sun. EMP, Electro Magnetic Pulse, can also occur as a direct result of human intervention. Nuclear weapons are known to cause massive EMP strikes when they detonate, and rumors about technologically advanced weaponry indicates that there may be specialized equipment capable of causing an EMP strike without detonating a nuclear weapon.

In America, the federal government owns and operates a series of weather related equipment designed for the specific purpose of manipulating the weather.

Several conspiracy theories abound about the true nature of what this equipment is capable of. H.A.A.R.P. is something you might want to research in depth. Unverified rumors indicate that this equipment can be used to harness the weather, manipulate it and use it as a weapon. It is also believed that this technology is either capable now, or will be capable in the very near future, of creating EMP like effects through acts of nature, targeting a specific location and manipulating the weather to cause the event. These people point to the increase of severity and frequency in weather related catastrophes around the world.

Regardless of what you believe, the fact that EMP can occur, with or without notice, natural or manmade, is one of the very real threats we as a global race, have absolutely no control over. Even if we couldn't manufacture EMP capable equipment ourselves, geological and historical evidence support the fact that these can, and have occurred, as a direct result of increased solar flare activity. When they occur, they knock out almost every form of electricity within the region. If they hit the right area, they can knock out an entire regional grid pattern and effect hundreds of millions of people who were not otherwise impacted by the event.

Surviving an EMP that is of a solar flare nature, may not be all that life threatening if you are properly prepared. If an EMP event of this sort cripples a very specific regional power grid, the collapse scenario will be of a temporary nature. You will still need to prepare as the electricity could be out for a period of days, weeks, or months, but will generally not be of the magnitude requiring a complete and total bug out, although that may be a personal preference of yours under these conditions. In order to protect your electrical equipment, consider **Faraday cages** as a sufficient protective method. These will keep your valuable appliances and computer equipment intact, even if the means of using them has been crippled. When the power comes back on, or you are able to generate your own, some of the equipment may be useable and serve a purpose. Alternative energy resources, such as wind, solar and hydro should be given some thought for these conditions as well.

If the EMP strike is the direct result of a massive solar flare event, or impact with an interstellar object, then the process of survival will be nothing short of what you have seem in the direst Hollywood renditions of what a post-apocalypse environment is likely to resemble. The zombies may not be flesh eating undead, but they will be out in force looking to secure goods wherever possible, by whatever means possible. They could become extremely violent and aggressive, showing little concern for their fellow man in their struggle to ensure they survive at all costs. These concerns will also apply to EMP strikes resulting from a nuclear strike. In this case the zombies may resemble the flesh eating undead, especially if they are caught above ground during the explosion and are exposed to harmful radiation contamination. They could pose a greater risk to those who were prepared to survive, which increases the concerns involved. Underground bunkers and environments are areas to focus on here as well.

Nuclear Strikes

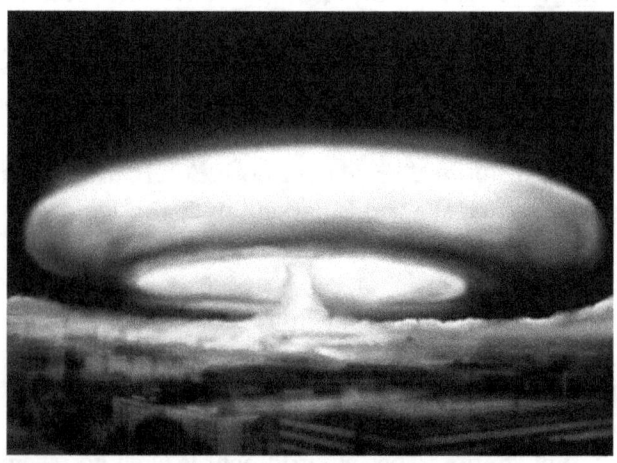

These are a concern, even for those who are not primarily focused on the EMP results. The majority of middle aged and older American generations, grew up during the Cold War Era. The threat of nuclear strikes was a common nightly news topic every time international relationships became strained, especially if those relationships were between the US and a country sympathetic to communist concepts. Today there are not only communist countries to be concerned with, but several countries in the Middle East that have long been adversaries of the American way of life, are beginning to develop their own nuclear technologies and weapons capabilities.

North Korea, has been all over the news recently, continuously spouting off rhetoric about launching nuclear capable missiles at targets of American interest, including our own homeland. They are a pesky little country with an enormous ally in the form of China. China is growing less and less enthused with the US government and would more than likely back North Korea's position if they did indeed decide to strike first. Pakistan in the Middle East, is a nuclear capable country with its own arsenal of nuclear tipped missiles. It is also a country constantly embroiled in turmoil and could fall under the direction of a dictator bent on destroying relationships with America. Iran, another Middle East country striving to develop nuclear technology and weaponry, has never been, and likely never will be, a trusted ally or member of the international community. Russia still has a stockpile of nuclear weapons left over from the Cold War Era. They are a country that has also begun to distance itself from the US government, standing up to the Obama administration at every available opportunity on the international scene, causing those in power in Washington D.C., look like nothing more than schoolyard bullies. All of this leads one to conclude that nuclear strikes are still a very real threat, maybe even more so now than during those old days of the Cold War Era.

Dirty bombs are another form of nuclear weapon that we should all start giving some very serious consideration to. With the increased levels of terrorism raging around the world, and the black market established for nuclear components, there exists a very real threat of unconventional nuclear weapons making an appearance at any time, at any location, with, or without warning. Rumors persist that dirty bombs are something the terrorist organizations around the globe are very capable of manufacturing and using. They do not have the traditional appearance of an industrialized nuclear warhead, which makes them harder to detect and intercept. These types of weapons do not necessarily need to be launched and arrive by airborne methods. They can be placed and exploded by remote trigger, hitting an area before it ever knew what was coming. They may not cause as much devastation and damage, but for those closest to ground zero or point of impact, will likely suffer many of the same consequences as if a conventional nuclear warhead had been used.

Nuclear strikes are not going to be a very easy thing to survive. Even if we do relocate to an underground shelter that is designed specifically for that purpose, depending on the nature of the event and the magnitude of international involvement, we could find ourselves surfacing to a planet no longer viable for growing crops and raising livestock. We could also find ourselves staring at a desolate landscape the natural resources of which are either destroyed, or at the very least too contaminated to consider using for years, decades, even centuries. The nuclear weapons we have today, make the ones used on Japan in WWII look like child's play. They are capable of exponentially greater damage, death and destruction. If they were to all be launched simultaneously, survival might require establishing an underground complex previously set-up and stocked to grow a garden and raise small farm animals. It also might require **living underground** for very lengthy periods of time. The nuclear fallout would turn Earth into our solar system's first snow globe, and the dust may not settle for months, or years.

Interstellar Impacts

This should also be a concern for anyone interested in survival. Our solar system is a massive pool of interstellar debris. We have asteroids, comets, meteors, meteorites, and things they don't have names for yet, all floating around just outside our atmosphere. Some of us have seen these things. We grow up calling them 'falling stars,' making a wish on them as they streak across the night sky. Believe it or not, they are just as active during the day, we just don't pick up on them as well with the naked eye, unless we know where to look and what to look for. We tend to think of these things as 'awe-inspiring,' 'mythical,' 'mystical,' and even 'magical.' What they truly are is warning signs that we have no control over how the universe operates. These little orbs bounce and glance off of the outer atmosphere for the most part, as they are too small to actually penetrate our planet's protective film.

Earth is not unfamiliar with interstellar impacts. There is more than enough evidence to prove that this planet has been hit by massive interstellar objects before. There is also evidence that several small impacts have occurred, depositing minerals in high content in areas where those minerals are not found naturally in the surrounding countryside. Earth can, and more than likely will, be hit by another massive interstellar object at some point and time in the future. Eventually our solar system's central star will self-destruct, sending shockwaves throughout the entire solar system. This will undoubtedly result in interstellar impact concerns for anyone on Earth when that day arrives. It may not be too far a stretch of the imagination to assume there could even be interplanetary collisions between Earth and its closest neighbor, the Moon.

Depending on the nature of the event. This may be all but impossible to survive. If the interstellar impact destroys the ozone and depletes the atmosphere of oxygen, only those living in subterranean environments capable of producing oxygen, growing food, and harvesting water from underground aquifers will survive. All above ground life forms will require oxygen generating equipment and space suits, as well as tethers in case gravity conditions are not as they once were.

Biological/Chemical Warfare

This should be another major concern for any and all living on this planet. Each country capable of making weapons and fending for itself, has the ability to manufacture chemical agents and biological weapons. They all know how to use them. They all stock and store the resources to manufacture them, and some are even advancing the methods by which they can be dispersed. This is not a conspiracy theory. It is indeed fact and should be a concern. All countries are basically governed by a handful of elected officials, all of which have the potential to abuse their positions and absorb power by force if necessary. Any one of them could use these capabilities at any time. We have seen this as recently as the Syrian Civil War.

There are some fairly interesting conspiracy theories surrounding chemical/biological weapons capabilities. Some people claim that the new strains of flu viruses we are seeing appear across the planet, are a direct result of scientific manipulation in a laboratory, while attempting to weaponize a potentially more lethal strain to be used against an adversary. Several people firmly believe that the AIDS virus was something brewed in a laboratory and accidentally released into the mainstream population, where it erupted and had pandemic attributes.

Regardless of whether or not any of these theories are true, chemical weapons and biological agents are in existence and can be used at any time. They are something we need to be aware of because they require special survival skills and gear in order to even be able to attempt resisting them. Just about anything can be used as a delivery vehicle for these types of weapons, so theoretically these could be used without anyone even knowing until affected individuals began showing external signs of contamination, which by then may be too late.

With the adequate forewarning, chemical and biological attacks can be survived, but without that forewarning, the chances of survival are dramatically reduced. Special **chemical suits**, **gas masks** and getting out of the affected area, are the order of the day and the first things to focus on.

Pandemics/Epidemics

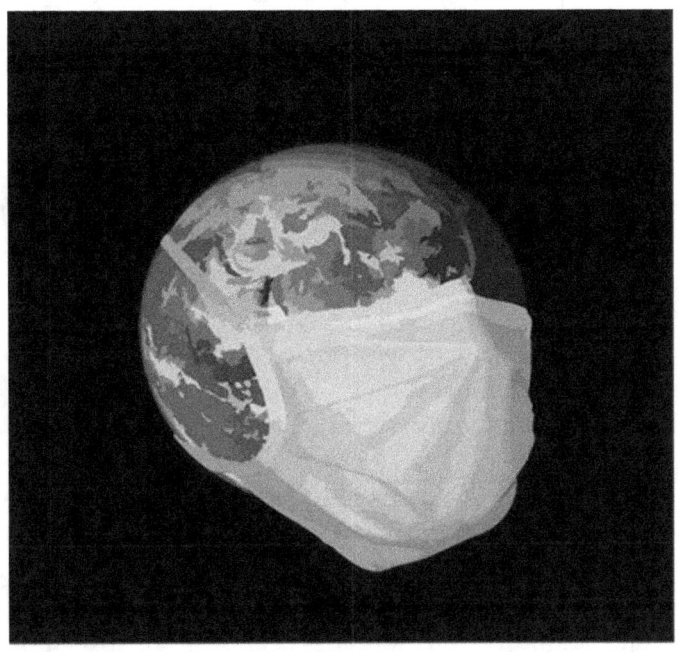

These are also very real possibilities. We have seen examples of both of these types of situations here on Earth, both in our lifetimes and throughout history. Pandemics are universal concerns. They fall into this category because they cannot be realistically controlled simply by closing a country's borders. The disease or effective agent is carried by a form of wildlife or other instrument, which is incapable of being controlled and quarantined by humankind. The Fukushima disaster and related leakage of trillions of gallons of harmful radioactive waste is a pandemic. It has had a seriously negative impact on the Pacific fishing industries, and thusly, all forms of seafood harvested from these areas.

Epidemics are localized events of a pandemic nature. They are controllable if attended to properly and timely before being allowed to erupt out of control and spread. Hurricane Katrina and the related aftermath conditions, in conjunction with improper measures on behalf of federal agencies such as FEMA, resulted in several illnesses achieving epidemic levels, simply because of the deplorable living conditions and communal sharing of commons areas.

Getting out of the affected area and ensuring the area you are headed to, isn't affected is the first order of business. If you are not sick, and none of your family are sick, then get out of Dodge before the region becomes quarantined. Quarantined is a medical term for Martial Law, it means the same thing, no leaving the cordoned off area for any reason. This is often done as a security measure by the controlling force implementing the quarantine as a method of **preventing the spread of the disease**. It is the same as a shelter in order place in a gun free zone, a recipe for disaster, especially for those not sick. If you get caught within a quarantined area, chances are you won't be getting out. The disease and sickness will be allowed to run their course while government scientists try to hurriedly come up with a medicine to combat the affects. This is not something that only happens in Hollywood movies. There are several third world countries where epidemics and quarantine conditions take place right now, in the present age.

Invasion by Foreign Ground Forces

This is an area that people are beginning to focus on more and more in the modern era. They are not afraid of a nuclear strike in conjunction with an invasion. Some of these people see the US military as stretched too thin and spread too far, in other international conflicts to be of much use if a foreign adversary elected to launch a ground/air invasion and attempt to take the country in a conventional ground war. There may be some merit to this concern. However, it should be noted that the US government has a very specified desire to conduct whatever wars or battles it is involved with on foreign soil, so chances are a ground invasion of the homeland would result in a counter invasion of the enemy country in question, along with a response force of National Guardsmen and individual patriots here at home.

An invasion of this nature would not necessarily come with a warning, and if it did, that warning would likely be of very little use. Foreign countries may, or may not, issue a formal declaration of war, indicating an invasion is imminent. Threats of war are usually just that, idle threats tossed around to make a few heads turn and take notice. This includes acts of terrorism which are at the very basis of their being, an act of war. We have seen these things happen on our own soil, some even resulting in the massive loss of life and property. Acts of terrorism are easily avoided by simply staying away from areas where high density pockets of population either exist, or are expected to be. These areas are high value targets for terrorists and their purposes. Stay as far away as possible from them and you increase your chances of not being added to a statistic sheet under the 'loss' column.

<u>Surviving a foreign ground force invasion</u> will take more effort, but will also require evacuating areas of high density population and for many of the same reasons. These would be the primary targets of any foreign ground force invading the homeland. They will strike where it will hurt the most and try to control and imprison as much of the population as possible. If you live in one of these areas, you may want to consider using underground waterways and sewer systems as your escape routes as there are likely to be less foreign troops looking for escapees and evacuees in these areas, at least during the initial phases of the invasion.

Alien Invasion

This is an area that is very difficult for most people to digest. Mathematically speaking, when all things we know to be true in the universe, are combined and correlated, it is an absolute impossibility that we are the only intelligent beings populating the multitude of stars, planets, and galaxies that we aware of.

This area is also ripe with conspiracy theories, from the Roswell incident, up to and including that the human race is subliminally controlled by an ancient subterranean reptilian life form. Attempting to describe the appropriate actions, survival skills and activities to take for an alien invasion is impossible, since we really have no historical data to draw from. Some people honestly believe that Earth has been visited for millions of years by beings from other planets. Several ancient civilizations worshipped gods and beings that they claim came from the stars. Several Native American tribal people also believe their ancestors were visited by 'star brothers,' and they claim these stories have been passed down from one generation to the next over the centuries, normally by tribal elders and shamans.

Surviving an alien invasion might also be impossible, given the fact we know very little about what their technologies allow them to be capable of accomplishing. It could realistically go either way. We could find ourselves invaded by a life form that closely resembles our own shapes, characteristics and habits, who have come here to help us become more advanced, or seeking a new host planet because theirs was destroyed. There are entirely too many possibilities to even try and cover accurately. Worst case scenario they show up, over power us with technology and weaponry, desecrate and destroy everything in sight and consume all of our natural resources, leaving our planet about as habitable as the Moon or Mars.

Conclusion

These are the Top 10 concerns for most survivalists and preppers. Again, this is not a complete list, nor has it been assembled in order of severity, frequency or related percentages of people concerned with a particular issue.

A lot of the information in this report sounds scary, maybe even crazy to some. All of these things are concerns because they can actually happen. They sound scary, daunting and overwhelming for one reason and one reason only; you are not properly prepared to handle them if they occur. You have come here looking to discover what you need to prepare for, and perhaps to unearth the general reasons to address these concerns. The material contained here was not intended to frighten you into prepping. It was designed to entice you to obtain a better understanding of why prepping is important; it is a confidence builder that allows you greater freedom and ability to take care of yourself.

Thankfully you have come to the right place. Here at Complete Survivalist we have plenty of informative material for you to absorb and educate yourself with. We have Gear Guides, Instruction Manuals, Webinars, a physical and digital print format for our magazine subscribers, as well as an archive that is a veritable treasure chest of additional survival information, compiled from some of the best authors and practitioners of survival skills, bushcrafting and prepping. Regardless of where you live, or what your primary concerns are, you will be able to find the information you need, all under one roof.

Life is far more liberating and enjoyable when you have the confidence of being prepared for any event that could happen and disrupt your ordinary way of life. You will eliminate a ton of mental stress you weren't even aware was causing a problem, simply by adjusting the way you live. Even if you never wind up needing to use a single survival skill, or piece of equipment, you will have the peace of mind that it is there if needed, and can be left to the next generation to ensure they are properly prepared during their lifetimes. Stop being a slave to conventional wisdom, start prepping and take back control over your life and that of your cherished family members!

DISCLAIMER AND/OR LEGAL NOTICES: Every effort has been made to accurately represent this book and it's potential. Results vary with every individual, and your results may or may not be different from those depicted. No promises, guarantees or warranties, whether stated or implied, have been made that you will produce any specific result from this book. Your efforts are individual and unique, and may vary from those shown. Your success depends on your efforts, background and motivation.

The material in this publication is provided for educational and informational purposes only and is not intended as medical advice. The information contained in this book should not be used to diagnose or treat any illness, metabolic disorder, disease or health problem. Always consult your physician or health care provider before beginning any nutrition or exercise program. Use of the programs, advice, and information contained in this book is at the sole choice and risk of the reader.